GREECE

By Johanna Barrow and
Kate Shoup

EXPLORING WORLD CULTURES

Cavendish Square

Published in 2023 by Cavendish Square Publishing, LLC
2544 Clinton Street, Buffalo, NY 14224

Second Edition

Library of Congress Cataloging-in-Publication Data

Names: Barrow, Johanna, author. | Shoup, Kate, author.
Title: Greece / Johanna Barrow and Kate Shoup.
Description: Buffalo, NY : Cavendish Square Publishing, [2023] | Series: Exploring world cultures | Includes index.
Identifiers: LCCN 2022025100 | ISBN 9781502667205 (library binding) | ISBN 9781502667199 (paperback) | ISBN 9781502667212 (ebook)
Subjects: LCSH: Greece--History--Juvenile literature.
Classification: LCC DF717 .B366 2023 | DDC 949.5--dc23/eng/20220525
LC record available at https://lccn.loc.gov/2022025100

Writers: Kate Shoup; Johanna Barrow (second edition)
Editor: Jennifer Lombardo
Copyeditor: Shannon Harts
Designer: Andrea Davison-Bartolotta

The photographs in this book are used by permission and through the courtesy of: Cover Max Topchii/Shutterstock.com; p. 4 airphoto.gr/Shutterstock.com; p. 5 A.B.G./Shutterstock.com; p. 6 Peter Hermes Furian/Shutterstock.com; p. 7 dinosmichail/Shutterstock.com; p. 8 tuulijumala/Shutterstock.com; p. 9 (main) Album/Alamy Stock Photo; p. 9 (background) carpetpatterndesigner/Shutterstock.com; p. 10 TTstudio/Shutterstock.com; p. 11 Truba7113/Shutterstock.com; p. 13 (top) Zebra-Studio/Shutterstock.com; p. 13 (bottom) Georgios Tsichlis/Shutterstock.com; p. 14 r.nagy/Shutterstock.com; p. 15 Ververidis Vasilis/Shutterstock.com; p. 16 Cavan-Images/Shutterstock.com; p. 17 a katz/Shutterstock.com; p. 18 Terry Harris/Alamy Stock Photo; p. 19 Isabella Pfenninger/Shutterstock.com; p. 20 Mazerath/Shutterstock.com; p. 21 Milan Gonda/Shutterstock.com; p. 22 zizou7/Shutterstock.com; p. 23 Ekaterina Pokrovsky/Shutterstock.com; p. 24 RHIMAGE/Shutterstock.com; p. 25 Roy Pedersen/Shutterstock.com; p. 26 Stock for you/Shutterstock.com; p. 27 Julia McGee/Shutterstock.com; p. 28 Toms Auzins/Shutterstock.com; p. 29 Elena Veselova/Shutterstok.com.

CPSIA compliance information: Batch #CW23CSQ: For further information contact Cavendish Square Publishing LLC at 1-877-980-4450.

Printed in the United States of America

CONTENTS

INTRODUCTION

When people think of Greece, they often think of beaches and islands. There's a reason for this: Greece is made up of thousands of islands, and no part of the country is more than 85 miles (137 kilometers) away from the ocean. However, 80 percent of the country is also covered in mountains that are great for hiking, skiing, and other outdoor activities.

Most Greek islands are tiny and have no one living on them.

Greece is often called the “cradle of Western civilization” because a lot of the things the Greeks invented have become part of life in the western part of the world. For example, the city of Athens is where theater was invented. Today, the city, which is the capital of Greece, has the most theaters of any city in the world. The Greeks also invented democracy, which is a system of government many countries—including the United States—use today. Most Greeks are very proud of their country and its long history.

Ancient Greek actors used masks to help the audience see what the characters were feeling.

GEOGRAPHY

The country that is the farthest south in Europe is Greece. It's separated into three parts. The first is the mainland, or the part that is connected to the rest of Europe. The second is the **peninsula** that is attached to the mainland. This part is called the Peloponnese. The third part of Greece is made up of thousands of islands.

Shown here is a map of Greece. The spellings of certain places are sometimes different depending on the source.

Ancient Greeks thought the gods lived on Mount Olympus.

There are mountains all over Greece. The tallest is called Mount Olympus, and it is on the mainland. In the winter, it snows in the mountains. In the rest of the country, winters are wet but not cold enough for snow. Summers in Greece are hot and dry. On average, **temperatures** range from 42 degrees Fahrenheit (5.5 degrees Celsius) in winter to 92°F (33°C) in the summer.

FACT!

People only live on about 200 of Greece's islands. The biggest island is called Crete. It was where the first Greeks lived.

MANY SEAS

Greece is surrounded by three bodies of water. The Aegean Sea is to the east of mainland Greece. The Ionian Sea is to the west. The Mediterranean Sea is to the south.

HISTORY

What is now the country of Greece started as a society on Crete around 3000 BCE. The people who lived there were called the Minoans. Around 1580 BCE, some Minoans moved to the mainland. Minoan civilization fell around 1600 BCE and was replaced by a group called the Mycenaeans. Their civilization lasted until about 1200 BCE.

FACT!

The ancient Greeks invented many things we use today, including alarm clocks, umbrellas, and maps.

Shown here is part of an ancient palace still standing on Crete.

Around 800 BCE, Greece started splitting itself into **city-states**. These city-states often fought with each other. Around 338 BCE, a leader named Philip II of Macedon combined them into one federation, or group. In 1453 CE, Greece was taken over by the Turks and made part of the Ottoman **Empire**. The Greeks fought and won a war for their independence in the 1800s.

THE DARK AGE

Around 1200 BCE, Greece entered what is now called its Dark Age. A lot of Greek **culture** was lost, including their writing system called Linear B. The Dark Age ended around 800 BCE.

Linear B (shown here) was lost in the Dark Age.

GOVERNMENT

Greece's official name is the Hellenic Republic. A republic is a kind of government where the power is held by the citizens and the leaders they elect. All Greek citizens 18 years old and older can vote in Greece's elections.

Greece's government is similar to that of the United States. It has three parts. The legislative branch writes new laws. In Greece, this branch is called the parliament. The judicial branch decides what the laws mean and what should happen to people who don't follow them. The executive branch **enforces** the laws.

Shown here is the Greek parliament building.

Greece's executive branch is made up of the president and the prime minister. The president is the head of the republic. The prime minister is in charge of the government.

FACT!

Greece had a king and queen from 1821 to 1974, with a break between 1924 and 1935.

Katerina Sakellaropoulou was elected president in 2020.

GREEK PARLIAMENT

The Greek world for parliament is *vouli*. This is also the name of the building where the 300 members of parliament meet. Parliamentary elections are held every four years.

THE ECONOMY

The most important part of Greece's economy—how the country makes its money—is tourism. This is when people visit a country to see what its culture is like. Tourists, or visitors, stay in hotels and buy food to eat. This brings a lot of money into the country.

Shipping has been an important part of Greece's economy since the time of the Minoans. Companies use Greek ships to carry items all over the world. Between 3 and 4 percent of all Greek employees, or workers, have jobs in shipping.

FACT!

Greece makes up about 18 percent of worldwide shipping.

There isn't a lot of good farmland in Greece, but many people do have farms. Some of the foods that are grown in Greece are pistachios, rice, olives, figs, tomatoes, and almonds. People also fish for sardines and anchovies.

The island of Santorini is popular with tourists.

Olives grow well in Greece.

TRADING WITH OTHER COUNTRIES

The countries Greece trades with the most are Italy, Germany, Turkey, Russia, and Iraq. Greece exports, or sends out, food, clothing, and machines. It imports, or brings in, different kinds of food, cars, and ships.

THE ENVIRONMENT

Greece used to have a lot of forests, but many trees have been cut down over the years. Today, the forests that are left are mainly in the mountains. Farms have also been a problem. People in the past did not use sustainable, or long-lasting, ways of farming. Today, there's not enough water because of this.

The air in Athens is very polluted.

FACT!

In April 2022, Greece opened one of the largest solar power plants in Europe.

In the 1970s, Greece built many new factories. The factories polluted the water and air. Cars and power plants burned materials that also polluted the air. However, Greece has been working for the last few years to clean up the environment, or natural world, and stop pollution. One way Greece is cutting down on pollution is by using clean energy sources that do not run on **fossil fuels**. These include wind, sun, and water power.

PROBLEMS IN ATHENS

Athens is Greece's largest city. A lot of environmental problems have come from there because of all the cars and factories. The pollution has given people a lot of health problems.

Climate change is causing more wildfires in Greece.

THE PEOPLE TODAY

Around 10.3 million people live in Greece. Most of them live in cities. About 3 million people live in Athens alone.

Most people who live in Greece come from the same **ethnic** group. They are called ethnic Greeks. They make up about 98 percent of the population. Ethnic Greeks tend to be very proud of where they come from. Other groups include Albanians, Aromanians, Romani, Turks, and Macedonians. These groups are quite small.

Shown here is the city of Kavala.

Some Americans can trace their family history back to Greece. Shown here is a Greek Independence Day parade in New York City.

FACT!

Because it's officially called the Hellenic Republic, Greek people call themselves "Hellenes."

In recent years, Greece has welcomed fewer immigrants, or people who come from other countries to live there. This is because the government has made it hard for some people to immigrate, including people who are trying to get away from war in their home country.

LEAVING GREECE

The Greek government spent too much money in the beginning of the 21st century. In 2009, this caused an economic **crisis**. A lot of people left Greece because they couldn't find jobs.

LIFESTYLE

The daily life of a Greek person living in a big city such as Athens is much different than the daily life of a farmer living on one of the smaller islands. However, some things connect all Greeks no matter where they live.

Greeks spend a lot of time outdoors, enjoying the beautiful weather the country is known for. Families often cook and eat meals outside together. Family is

Meals are often shared with family in Greece.

very important to Greeks. Dancing is also something many Greeks do for fun when they get together.

Greeks care a lot about **tradition**. In most cases, this is a nice way to keep their culture alive. However, ideas about what is traditional sometimes stop women from getting the same treatment as men at home and at work.

FACT!
Women in Greece did not get the right to vote until 1952.

SUPERSTITIONS

Greeks tend to be superstitious, which means they believe in doing things to keep bad luck away. Some of these include spitting on loved ones, never throwing away bread, and never handing someone a knife.

Greeks use these glass beads to keep away the "evil eye," which brings bad luck.

RELIGION

People all over the world still tell stories about ancient Greek gods and goddesses. Ancient Greeks believed in 12 main gods. Zeus was the king of all gods. His wife was a goddess named Hera. Other gods and goddesses controlled things such as the sea, hunting, love, and death.

People still visit the temples the ancient Greeks built to honor their gods and goddesses.

SPREADING RELIGION

Greece and Italy have each controlled the other at certain points in history. For this reason, their religions mixed. Ancient Romans had the same gods and goddesses as the Greeks, but with different names.

Today, most Greeks—about 90 percent—are Christian. Their type of Christianity is called Eastern Orthodoxy. It's led by the Greek Orthodox Church. However, the country has no official religion, or faith. By law, Greeks are free to practice any religion they wish. About 10 percent of Greeks follow one of a small group of other religions including Islam, Judaism, and Catholicism. Also among this 10 percent are people who don't follow any religion at all.

FACT!

Greece and Russia are the countries with the highest number of Eastern Orthodox followers in the world.

Greek Orthodox churches are often beautifully decorated.

LANGUAGE

The Greek language has been used for 34 centuries, making it one of the oldest in the world. The Greek alphabet does not use the same letters as the English one, which is called the Latin alphabet. Instead, it includes letters such as Δ (delta), ∏ (pi), and ∑ (sigma). Many of these letters are also used in mathematics.

Α α alpha	Β β beta	Γ γ gamma	Δ δ delta
Ε ε epsilon	Ζ ζ zeta	Η η eta	Θ θ theta
Ι ι iota	Κ κ kappa	Λ λ lambda	Μ μ mu
Ν ν nu	Ξ ξ xi	Ο ο omicron	Π π pi
Ρ ρ rho	Σ σ ς sigma	Τ τ tau	Υ υ upsilon
Φ φ phi	Χ χ chi	Ψ ψ psi	Ω ω omega

The Greek alphabet was reinvented after the Dark Age.

The Greek language has many forms called dialects. For example, in the Peloponnese, some people speak an ancient dialect called Tsakonian. The official dialect the country uses is called Standard Modern Greek. Because Greece is part of a group of countries called the European Union (EU), Standard Modern Greek is one of the EU's official languages.

Other languages that are spoken in Greece include Macedonian, Albanian, and Turkish. However, not many people speak these languages.

FACT!

Tsakonian is closer to ancient Greek than it is to modern Greek.

Greek words can be written with Latin letters. This is called Romanization.

COVID-19 VARIANTS

Different forms, or variants, of the sickness known as COVID-19 are named after Greek letters. These include Alpha, Beta, Delta, and Omicron.

ARTS AND FESTIVALS

The Greeks have been making art since their civilization began. They are known for their pottery and **sculptures**. The ancient Greek style is very distinctive, or easy to recognize.

Early Greeks also wrote long poems, called epics, and played music on instruments they invented, including the pan flute. Today, Greeks still enjoy music and poetry. They also enjoy going to the movies, watching TV, and visiting **museums**.

FACT!
The Acropolis Museum in Athens has many objects from ancient Greece.

This pottery shows the distinctive Greek art style.

Greeks celebrate several holidays. These include Greek Independence Day (March 25), Labor Day (May 1), and Ohi Day (October 28). On Ohi Day, Greeks remember the day in 1940 when the Greek prime minister did not let the Italian army invade Greece during the Greco-Italian War. Greeks also celebrate Christian holidays, including Christmas and Easter.

Greece has festivals where people eat, drink, and dance.

A MODERN GREEK MOVIE

In 2002, a Greek woman named Nia Vardalos wrote and starred in the movie *My Big Fat Greek Wedding*. It showed many non-Greek people Greek traditions and culture in a funny way.

FUN AND PLAY

Like theater, sports have always been a large part of Greek culture. In fact, the early Greeks invented the Olympic Games. They were held for nearly 12 centuries. Emperor Theodosius I of Rome banned them in 393 CE because they were not Christian.

FACT!

After more than 1,500 years, the Olympics were brought back in 1896 as a way to get different countries to get along.

Since ancient times, Greeks have enjoyed wrestling, running, and **gymnastics**. Today, they also enjoy basketball and soccer, which they call "football." In fact, the country's

Today, more than 200 countries take part in the Olympics.

national sport is football. Many Greeks also travel to the mountains for activities such as skiing and hiking.

The Greeks also like playing games. Ancient Greeks played several dice and board games. Many games like these are still played today. Greece's national board game is called Tavli. It uses a backgammon board, but it has different rules.

OLYMPIC HISTORY

The first written record of the Olympics is from 776 BCE, but they might have started even earlier. They were held every four years in honor of Zeus. Only Greeks took part in the games.

Shown here is a game of Tavli.

FOOD

Greek food is loved by people around the world. Many Greek dishes are made with a lot of vegetables and not very much meat. Some foods that are strongly Greek are feta cheese, which is made from sheep and goat's milk, and tzatziki, which is a kind of sauce made with yogurt and cucumber.

WHERE'S THE BEEF?

When Greeks do cook meat, they often choose fish or lamb. They do not eat a lot of beef because Greece does not have enough land that is good for raising cows.

Because Greece is surrounded by water, fish is often part of meals.

Greek cooks use a lot of olive oil, lemon juice, herbs, and spices. Often, meals are served with a type of flat bread called pita bread. One popular dish that the Greeks have eaten since ancient times is a soup called fasolada. It is made with white beans, vegetables, and olive oil. Many Greek desserts are made with honey. One of the most popular is called baklava. It is made with a special flaky dough called phyllo.

FACT!

Greek food is very similar to Turkish food because of the years Greece was part of the Ottoman Empire.

Greek baklava (shown here) is mainly made with walnuts, while Turkish baklava more often uses a kind of nut called pistachio.

GLOSSARY

city-state: A self-governing state made up of a city and surrounding lands.

climate change: Change in Earth's weather caused by human activity.

crisis: A difficult or dangerous situation that needs serious attention.

culture: The habits, beliefs, and traditions of a particular people, place, or time.

empire: A group of territories or people under one ruler.

enforce: To make sure people obey the law.

ethnic: Relating to groups of people with common characteristics and customs.

fossil fuel: A fuel (such as coal, oil, or natural gas) formed in the earth from dead plants or animals.

gymnastics: A sport that includes rolls, flips, and other moves often performed on rings or bars.

museum: A building in which things of interest are displayed.

peninsula: A landmass that is surrounded by water on three sides.

sculpture: A work of art made from stone, metal, or clay.

temperature: How hot or cold something is.

tradition: A belief or custom handed down from one generation to another.

FIND OUT MORE

Books

Finan, Catherine C. *Ancient Greece*. Minneapolis, MN: Bearport Publishing, 2022.

Leaf, Christina. *Greece*. Minneapolis, MN: Bellwether Media, 2020.

Website

***National Geographic Kids*: Greece**
kids.nationalgeographic.com/geography/countries/article/greece
Learn more cool facts about Greece.

Video

YouTube: Kids Try Greek Food
www.youtube.com/watch?v=GKGpEW1l9ks
Four kids taste-test Greek food and give their thoughts about it.

Publisher's note to educators and parents: Our editors have carefully reviewed these websites to ensure that they are suitable for students. Many websites change frequently, however, and we cannot guarantee that a site's future contents will continue to meet our high standards of quality and educational value. Be advised that students should be closely supervised whenever they access the internet.

INDEX